Newton's Rainbow

To Obi and Arrow,
who are curious —K.H.

Farrar Straus Giroux Books for Young Readers
An imprint of Macmillan Publishing Group, LLC
175 Fifth Avenue, New York 10010

Text copyright © 2017 by Kathryn Lasky
Pictures copyright © 2017 by Kevin Hawkes
All rights reserved
Color separations by Bright Arts (H.K.) Ltd.
Printed in China by RR Donnelley Asia Printing Solutions Ltd.,
Dongguan City, Guangdong Province
First edition, 2017
1 3 5 7 9 10 8 6 4 2

mackids.com

Library of Congress Cataloging-in-Publication Data
Names: Lasky, Kathryn, author. | Hawkes, Kevin, illustrator.
Title: Newton's rainbow : the revolutionary discoveries of a young scientist
  / Kathryn Lasky ; pictures by Kevin Hawkes.
Description: First edition. | New York : Farrar Straus Giroux, 2017 |
  Audience: 4–8.
Identifiers: LCCN 2016020102 | ISBN 9780374355135 (hardcover)
Subjects: LCSH: Newton, Isaac, 1642–1727—Juvenile literature.
Classification: LCC QC16.N7 L37 2017 | DDC 530.092 [B]—dc23
LC record available at https://lccn.loc.gov/2016020102

Our books may be purchased in bulk for promotional, educational,
or business use. Please contact your local bookseller or the Macmillan
Corporate and Premium Sales Department at (800) 221-7945 ext. 5442
or by e-mail at MacmillanSpecialMarkets@macmillan.com.

Newton's Rainbow

The Revolutionary Discoveries of a Young Scientist

Kathryn Lasky

Pictures by Kevin Hawkes

Farrar Straus Giroux
New York

THE TINIEST BABY

On Christmas Day over three hundred years ago, in a village in England, a baby was born too early. The midwives who helped deliver him had never seen such a tiny baby, so little that one said he could fit into a quart pot. No one expected him to live. But he did. His name was Isaac Newton.

Isaac's life was sad from the start. A few months before he was born, his father died. When Isaac was three, his mother, Hannah, remarried. His stepfather insisted that Isaac live not with them but with his grandparents.

SCHOOLBOY SCIENTIST

Isaac was tiny not only as a baby but as a child as well. He never grew very tall. He kept to himself because the bigger boys in school bullied him. He was described as a "sober, silent, thinking lad." But he did learn how to read and write, which neither his stepfather nor his mother could do.

In 1653, when Isaac was eleven, his stepfather died, and his mother returned with three new children to live with Isaac and his grandparents. Isaac, however, was soon sent to a new school in the village of Grantham. There, he boarded with the village apothecary, William Clark.

The shelves of the apothecary were crammed with the wonders from which medicines and remedies were brewed. There were jars filled with strange-colored fluids. There were pots stuffed with spiderwebs for wounds and powders for warts, boils, and toothaches.

Mr. Clark used bloodsucking leeches to treat fevers and infected cuts, and the livers of green frogs and lizards for digestive problems. In addition, he had a collection of all kinds of herbs, leaves, bark, and seeds to concoct remedies for ailments.

These jars and pots offered Isaac his introduction to chemistry. Quietly he would watch Mr. Clark mix and blend potions. Isaac began keeping a notebook of remedies. One required the patient to drink a mixture of mint, the bitter herb wormwood, and three hundred headless millipedes "well beaten with ale."

Unlike Isaac's own family, William Clark was an educated man. He owned many books, and Isaac began to read—a lot! One book was about Galileo, who was considered the world's first astronomer. Galileo had died the year that Isaac was born.

GALILEO GALILEI (1564–1642) was an Italian physicist, mathematician, astronomer, and philosopher. He made many improvements to the telescope and was called the father of modern observational astronomy. He discovered the four largest satellites of Jupiter, which were named the Galilean Moons in his honor. But he also got into big trouble when he supported the theory that the earth orbited the sun. He was attacked by the Catholic church for his beliefs. Tried and found guilty, he was ordered to be held under house arrest for the rest of his life.

Even though Isaac was a thinking lad who read about Galileo and studied herbs and medicines, he was not the kind of student that his schoolmasters appreciated. He was at the bottom of his class in the Grantham grammar school. His teachers thought he was "idle" and "inattentive." And his classmates ignored the quiet and serious boy.

But two things happened that changed school for Isaac. The first was that he beat up the school bully in a fight—even though the bully was much bigger. It was not muscle that made Isaac the winner but his spirit and energy. His schoolmates were amazed that this shrimpy boy could vanquish someone with a higher class ranking. After this incident Isaac's academic performance improved.

The second incident that changed things for Isaac was a jumping competition. With his short, rather stubby legs Isaac was not expected to do well. But the day of the contest was a windy one. Isaac waited and observed patiently. The other contestants might have wondered: Why is he waiting? Is he scared? But finally, when Isaac detected an extra-strong gust blowing his way, he jumped, and when he jumped he caught the wind and sailed off the mark in a spectacular, lovely high arc. He won the contest.

At this point in his young life, Isaac most likely did not even know the word "physics," but he was already using the laws of motion, laws that he would later explain and that form the basis of modern physics. In centuries that followed, this new physics would focus on the study of atoms—the smallest particles in nature—and on the rules that govern matter and energy in the physical world.

Still, Isaac Newton was not thought of as especially smart. His teachers used the words "cunning" and "crafty," but never "clever." Although he kept to himself, he was rarely lonely. He had plenty to think about and was always occupied. He began drawing all sorts of things with charcoal—birds, ships, animals, plants, a picture of King Charles, and another of the poet John Donne. Often he drew these pictures directly onto the walls of his room. He also carved his name in his school desk; in fact, he carved it into every school desk he ever sat in as a boy.

A Curious Mind

Desks were not all that Isaac carved. When he was nine, he carved a sundial on the wall of his house. Then when he lived with the Clarks, he began making sundials—some on walls, some by tying strings to pegs stuck in the garden. With these shadow clocks, as they were often called, he could trace the path of the sun by following the shadows cast on the clock face. He spent endless hours measuring the shadows on different days as the seasons progressed and the sun rose and set at different angles to the earth. Isaac became so alert to the movement of shadows that it was said he could walk into a room and, without ever looking at a clock, know the time. It was perhaps this that led to his curiosity about the movement of the planets.

Other inventions included a miniature mill for grinding corn. Windmills were uncommon in that part of England because there were so many rivers and streams for water mills. So when one was built in Grantham, the entire village turned out to see how it worked. On the blades of the windmill's tower, canvas had been stretched to catch the wind. Isaac watched these four long sails begin to turn as the breeze rose. He went home to make a tiny model, but he came up with a new idea.

Instead of wind power, which he felt was unreliable, he decided on mouse power. Isaac attached a string to a mouse's tail and put the mouse on a treadmill. When he tugged on the string, the mouse ran. Now people came to look at this tiny mill built by the crafty, cunning Isaac. A farmer even gave him some corn for the mouse miller to grind.

There were more models: Dollhouse furniture for William Clark's daughter, Catherine, who was perhaps the only child with whom Isaac became friendly. Kites of all shapes and sizes, because Isaac wanted to see what flew best in which kinds of wind. Once, he decided to attach a lantern with a lighted candle to the tail of his kite and fly it at night. Isaac reported that the neighbors were "wonderfully affrighted" by the strange light appearing in the sky.

By the time Isaac was sixteen, he had built not only countless sundials, but a water clock and a small four-wheeled vehicle that he could climb into and power by turning a crank. He had invented new inks using odd things, like the blood of sheep. Gradually people, and even a teacher, Mr. Stokes, began to realize that Isaac was more than cunning and crafty. He was clever. At just about this time, however, his mother said Isaac needed to end his school days and come home to help with the farm.

THE ABSENTMINDED FARMER

Isaac was a complete disaster as a farmer. He was beyond idle and inattentive. The entire time he tended sheep or minded cattle he was still thinking about waterwheels and windmills and the movement of the sun and the stars and the planets in their orbits. Meanwhile, the sheep wandered off into the neighbors' fields to eat their grass and grain. Once, when going to market, Isaac got off his horse to go up a hill, thinking to make it easier for the horse. It turned out to be very easy for the horse, as Isaac forgot to get back on at the top of the hill—and for the next five miles! Another time, the horse slipped out of its harness when being led by Isaac, who didn't notice and just continued to walk, still holding the bridle.

Finally Isaac's teacher Mr. Stokes convinced Isaac's mother that her son's gifts and talents were wasted on the farm. He needed to finish his schooling so he could go to university. When he departed for school, it was said that even the servants rejoiced. They believed that he was fit for nothing but book learning.

A Pound of Candles, a Chamber Pot, Ink, and a Brain

Isaac's mother did not like the idea of education. She refused to give him any money when he left to enroll at Trinity College, one of several colleges that made up Cambridge University. Poor students like Isaac were called "subsizars." To earn their way, they were required to act as servants for the wealthier students and teachers. So the only belongings that Isaac arrived with were a lock for his desk, a notebook, ink, a pound of candles, and a chamber pot—a large bowl used at night as a toilet.

He had roommate problems from the start. The first one liked to go to pubs and parties throughout the night. Isaac found another student, John Wickins, who shared his dislike for parties and "disorderly companions." Newton and Wickins decided to "chum together," which meant sharing a room. Although it was said that they were never really close friends, they roomed together for many years at Trinity College.

Isaac studied the usual subjects—Greek, Latin, Hebrew, religion, and the different branches of science, including mathematics and astronomy, which were together called philosophy. Aristotle was a Greek philosopher whose theories were much studied. He believed, for example, that the heavier of two different weights when dropped from the same height would hit the ground first. But he never tested it. Galileo did test this theory—and proved Aristotle wrong. One of the reasons Isaac liked Galileo was that he experimented, trying through measuring and observation to prove things right instead of just saying they were right.

One of Galileo's experiments was to drop two cannonballs of different weights from the top of the famous Leaning Tower of Pisa in Italy to demonstrate that both fell at the same speed. This proved that weight did not matter in relation to speed.

Isaac, too, was an experimenter. He had little patience with talkers. From the time he made his first sundials and won the jumping contest by timing the wind gusts, Isaac knew that action, experimentation, and observation would help him unlock the secrets of the universe. During one lecture on Aristotle, Isaac stopped taking notes and wrote at the top of a fresh page in Latin: "I am a friend of Plato, I am a friend of Aristotle, but Truth is my greater friend."

Amicus Plato amicus Aristoteles magis amica veritas

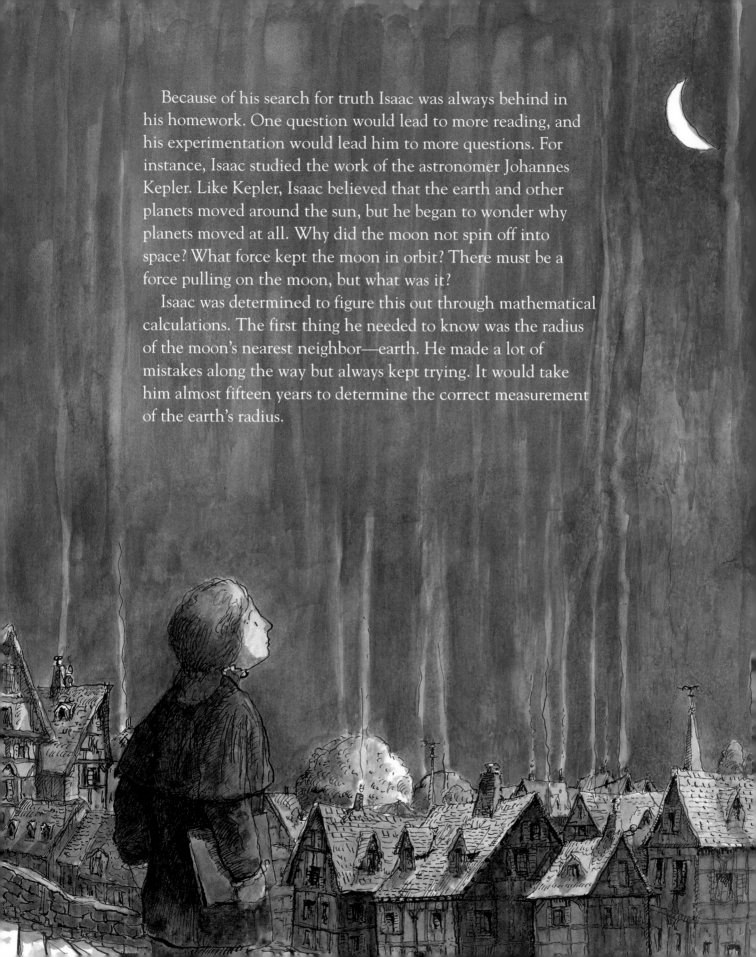

Because of his search for truth Isaac was always behind in his homework. One question would lead to more reading, and his experimentation would lead him to more questions. For instance, Isaac studied the work of the astronomer Johannes Kepler. Like Kepler, Isaac believed that the earth and other planets moved around the sun, but he began to wonder why planets moved at all. Why did the moon not spin off into space? What force kept the moon in orbit? There must be a force pulling on the moon, but what was it?

Isaac was determined to figure this out through mathematical calculations. The first thing he needed to know was the radius of the moon's nearest neighbor—earth. He made a lot of mistakes along the way but always kept trying. It would take him almost fifteen years to determine the correct measurement of the earth's radius.

Isaac would have considered JOHANNES KEPLER (1571–1630) a truth-seeker like himself. The work of this German astronomer was of special interest to him. Kepler had figured out that the shape of a planet's orbit was an ellipse, or flattened oval. He had also figured out how the speed at which a planet travels depends on its distance from the sun. And lastly, Kepler worked out the specific mathematical relationship between a planet's distance from the sun and the length of time it takes the planet to orbit the sun. These became known as Kepler's Three Laws of Planetary Motion.

Isaac found these three laws very exciting—not simply for what they did say but for what they did not. The laws described the motion of the planets but not what caused them to move in the first place.

Isaac took notes on everything he read and even changed his handwriting so he could write faster. The room he shared with Wickins became more of a laboratory than a bedroom or study. Its shelves were crammed with bottles of chemicals, instruments, beakers, and small burners for experimenting with gases. He made long lists of things he wanted to explore and learn about.

Here is a short part of one of those lists:

Sleep

Soul

Tides

Motion

Time

Matter

Sunn, Stars & Planets & Comets

Isaac loved watching the night sky and would often forget to eat. His pet cat would gobble the untouched food on his plate. As Isaac got thinner and thinner, his cat grew fatter and fatter.

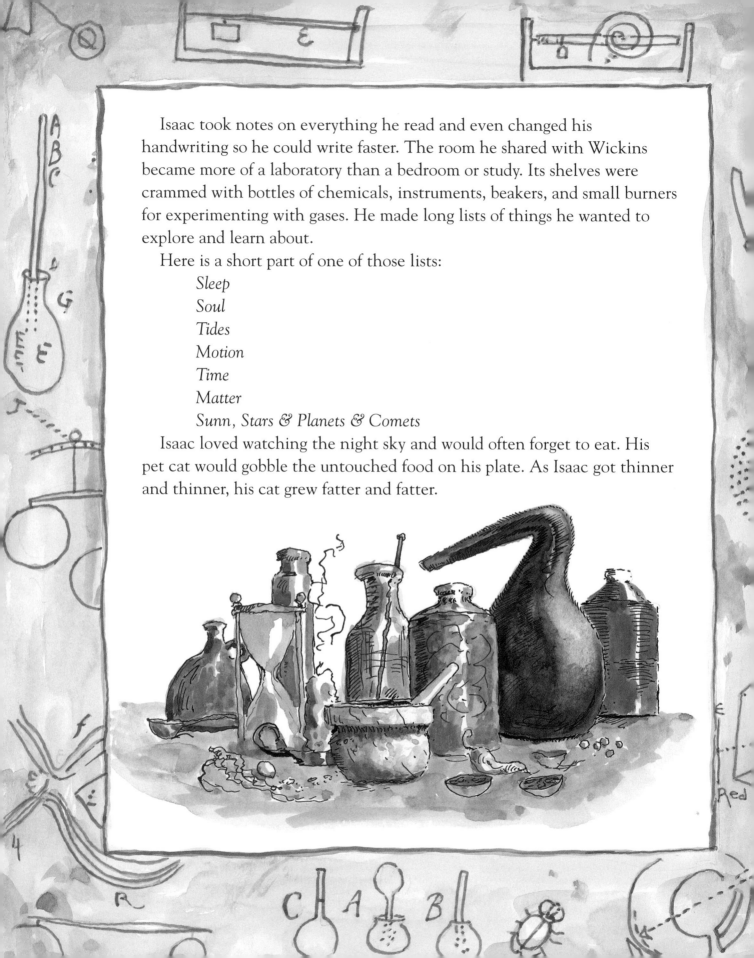

At Cambridge, it was mathematics that interested Isaac the most. But when he arrived at university, his knowledge of math was very limited. On an early geometry test he could not answer a single question. But soon he taught himself not only the classical geometry of the Greeks—which examines the nature of relationships between points, lines, angles, curves, surfaces, and solids—but a newer and much more complicated geometry that had developed a few decades before he was born.

Isaac had been at Cambridge University for almost four years and was just short of earning his degree, when a rat got off a ship and changed everything.

ANNUS MIRABILIS

It would not be fair to blame it all on the rat. It was really the flea that alighted on the rat that boarded the Dutch ship that sailed to England with bales of cotton. The rat scurried off the ship with the flea still tucked somewhere in its fur, all cozy and comfy. The flea by this time had most likely reproduced and had not only children but grandchildren and great-grandchildren and even great-great-grandchildren.

These fleas that lived on black rats carried a deadly disease. It was called the bubonic plague, and thus this plague came to London. Within three days of a person's being bitten by an infected flea, a black pustule, or pimple, formed on the skin. This was followed by "bubos," large swellings in the neck, armpits, and groin. Then came a headache, vomiting, chills, delirium—or "madness," as it was called—and, finally, death.

The bubonic plague first struck during the winter of 1664–65 in the dock areas of London, where poor workers lived in crowded, filthy conditions. It began to spread rapidly when the warmer weather of spring and the hot weather of summer arrived. By September, seven thousand people a week were dying from the plague in London alone. Almost every other house had a cross painted on it, indicating that its residents had been struck by the plague. Drivers of carts wound their way through empty streets shouting, "Bring out your dead." The dead were buried in pits.

Although Cambridge University was fifty miles away from London, it was decided in August of 1665 to close all the colleges, including Trinity. Isaac had left in June and would not return for almost two years.

But for Isaac the year of death became the miraculous year. He even called it that: *annus mirabilis*. For it was not at Cambridge University but at his mother's house in Woolsthorpe that Isaac Newton made three of the greatest breakthroughs of modern science.

The first was his formulation of the law of gravity, the guiding principle of physics.

The second was the development of calculus, a new method of mathematics. With calculus one could figure out the rate of change over time of something as ordinary as the path of a ball thrown into the air—or the jump made by a boy on a windy day!

And, finally, he made a giant step forward in understanding the mysteries of light and color—the very secret of rainbows. Luckily, Isaac's mother did not insist on him minding sheep. Instead, he sat for long periods in the garden minding his mind, thinking, wondering, reflecting on the force that keeps stars in the sky and planets in their orbits.

The story is that he was napping in the garden when an apple fell from a tree, bopping him on the head, and—*boing!*—Isaac Newton began to develop the theory of gravitation.

Here is what's true. There was a garden. There was an apple tree. The apple really did fall. Isaac was not asleep. He may have been thinking with his eyes closed. We might imagine that he was thinking about Kepler's laws of planetary motion, given what came next—but then again, he might have been thinking about what was for supper, or that it had been a week since his last bath. (People didn't bathe much back then.) No one knows for sure, and there were no witnesses. According to a 1752 book about Isaac's life, written by a friend, he was not actually hit on the head by an apple. The book says, rather, that the theory was "occasion'd by the fall of an apple."

Isaac had been thinking about gravity for a long time. And what he thought when he saw the apple was: Why doesn't that apple fall up, or sideways? Why down? He wondered about the force that made it do this, and then he looked up into the sky. Perhaps, since it was afternoon, he saw only the faint outline of the moon, but he could imagine the night sky and all the stars, and he wondered if such a force could stretch out into the heavens and account for the orbits of the planets around the sun and the moon around the earth. He began to understand that if the moon wasn't moving, it would most certainly crash into the earth, like the apple.

The questions unanswered by Kepler's laws of motion haunted him as he looked at this apple. There must be a force exerted on the moon, a force opposed to gravity that kept it in its orbit. He knew then that there must be rules of force that governed the planets and other bodies in motion. Isaac would begin to formulate these rules, which would be known as the laws of motion. Later, he would combine these laws with his own law of universal gravitation. Together they became the basis for modern physics.

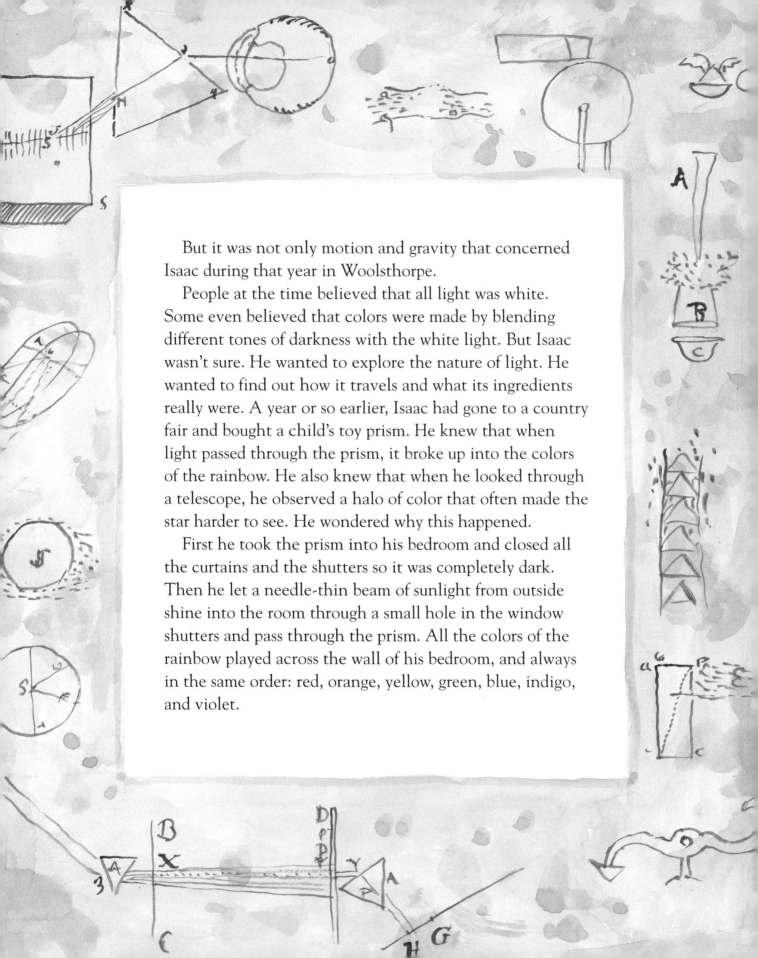

But it was not only motion and gravity that concerned Isaac during that year in Woolsthorpe.

People at the time believed that all light was white. Some even believed that colors were made by blending different tones of darkness with the white light. But Isaac wasn't sure. He wanted to explore the nature of light. He wanted to find out how it travels and what its ingredients really were. A year or so earlier, Isaac had gone to a country fair and bought a child's toy prism. He knew that when light passed through the prism, it broke up into the colors of the rainbow. He also knew that when he looked through a telescope, he observed a halo of color that often made the star harder to see. He wondered why this happened.

First he took the prism into his bedroom and closed all the curtains and the shutters so it was completely dark. Then he let a needle-thin beam of sunlight from outside shine into the room through a small hole in the window shutters and pass through the prism. All the colors of the rainbow played across the wall of his bedroom, and always in the same order: red, orange, yellow, green, blue, indigo, and violet.

He next tried another experiment. This experiment used two pinholes and two prisms. The first pinhole was the one in the shutters. As before, light from the pinhole passed through the first prism. From that prism, all the colors were refracted onto a wooden board. This board had the second pinhole, allowing only one of the seven colors to pass through it to the second prism.

People had long believed that it was the prism coloring the light. But Isaac's experiment proved this was not true, for if it had been, all the colors would have returned after the light passed through the second prism. They did not.

Isaac had shown that prisms did not color the light, and that light itself was composed of seven different colors.

And if this wasn't proof enough, he tried one more experiment. This time he again used two prisms, but placed the second one upside down. Now the first prism split the beam of white light into seven separate colors and the second prism brought them back together to make white light once again.

Isaac had discovered the secret of the rainbow, and it was not a pot of gold at the end. A rainbow was the seven different colors of "white light" after passing through the tiny prisms formed by raindrops in the atmosphere.

Isaac's *annus mirabilis* stretched into eighteen months and included more accomplishments. Then, on the first night of September 1666, a fire broke out in a bakery in Pudding Lane in London. By the next morning, a wind had risen and the fire spread throughout the city. Fed by the crowded thatched-roof wooden buildings, it became so intense that no one could get near it. For four days and four nights the city burned, destroying over 13,000 houses and 87 churches, including St. Paul's Cathedral. It jumped the Fleet River and threatened to consume the court of King Charles II at Whitehall. But finally the wind died down, and the firefighters were successful in quenching the flames.

There was one blessing that came with the fire. Not only were houses and other buildings destroyed, but the rats that carried the diseased fleas were destroyed as well. The plague was finally over.

Six months later, Isaac returned to Trinity College at Cambridge University.

A Scholar's Gown

Soon after returning to Trinity College, Isaac took the examinations that would determine his future. If he did well, he could become a fellow of the college and spend the rest of his life as a scholar at the university—studying, giving lectures, and helping students. That year, there were only nine openings, so he would have to do exceedingly well.

For four days Isaac was asked to write and answer questions. On October 1 a tolling bell summoned the candidates to the chapel, where they would learn their destiny. Newton was one of the nine chosen. He immediately went into the town of Cambridge and bought twelve yards of dark blue fabric, the color of Trinity College's scholars' gowns.

Perhaps since he was now a fellow with a guaranteed income, he felt he could expand his household items beyond the chamber pot, candles, ink, and notebook with which he had arrived. He bought a new bed, a tablecloth, and six napkins. For some reason, of all the colors of the rainbow that he had managed to splinter apart, he became obsessed with crimson, a deep shade of red. In an uncharacteristic splurge he bought new cushions, a bedspread, curtains, and carpets in his favorite color. For the rest of his life he would surround himself with color, but it was usually crimson.

Isaac Newton lived to the age of eighty-four, but he never became an especially sociable man. He never married and he had few friends. He lived in his imagination and dared to test the things he imagined through experiment. To further explore his theories of the color spectrum, he blew soap bubbles through a clay pipe and began to grasp how, when light fell on the bubble, the thin film of the soap functioned as a kind of liquid prism. And if he was not blowing bubbles, he was figuring out mathematical solutions for the elliptical paths of planets. In truth, Newton had figured out the solution for this problem many years earlier, but he had lost the papers with his calculations. It was only when Edmund Halley, the famous astronomer, begged him to write it down that he finally explained it in a nine-page document written in Latin, the language used by scholars in their writings at that time.

Newton did not like to share his ideas; he guarded them as a miser might guard his pile of gold. Yet for all his cantankerousness, he was generous in giving credit to others. However, his generosity for the most part extended to scientists who were already dead, like Galileo and Kepler.

When asked how he could see and understand things that others could not, he would reply, "If I have seen further, it is because I have stood on the shoulders of giants." And it was on the shoulders of Isaac Newton that future scientists, including the greatest scientist of the twentieth century, Albert Einstein, would perch to peer beyond the secrets of the rainbow to those of space and time and the very origins of our universe.

BIBLIOGRAPHY

Anderson, Margaret J. *Isaac Newton: The Greatest Scientist of All Time* (Berkeley Heights, N.J.: Enslow Publishers, 1996). For readers aged nine and up, a sturdy biography rich in details about Newton's life and revolutionary scientific achievements.

Aughton, Peter. *Newton's Apple: Isaac Newton and the English Scientific Renaissance* (London: Weidenfeld & Nicholson, 2003).

Cambridge University Library. *Footprints of the Lion: Isaac Newton at Work* (www.lib.cam.ac.uk/exhibitions/Footprints_of_the_Lion). An online biography that serves as a gateway to the library's extensive collections of Newton's papers and other material.

Clark, David, and Stephen P. H. Clark. *Newton's Tyranny: The Suppressed Scientific Discoveries of Stephen Gray and John Flamsteed* (New York: W. H. Freeman, 2000).

Defoe, Daniel. *A Journal of the Plague Year.* Defoe's fascinating 1722 account, published three years after his famous novel *Robinson Crusoe*, of the bubonic plague outbreak in London in 1665— Newton's *annus mirabilis*.

Isaac Newton Institute for Mathematical Sciences. *Isaac Newton Resources* (www.newton.cam.ac.uk/newton). A trove of resources about Newton for all ages.

Krull, Kathleen. *Isaac Newton* (New York: Viking, 2006). For readers in grades five through eight, an acclaimed and colorful biography, amusingly illustrated by Boris Kulikov, that doesn't shy away from the darker, contradictory side of Newton's character and achievements.

Stuckeley, William. *Memoirs of Sir Isaac Newton's Life* (www.newtonproject.sussex.ac.uk/view/texts/normalized/OTHE00001). Reverend Stuckeley's 1752 memoir of his friend Isaac Newton's life is an early source for the story of the falling apple: "After dinner, the weather being warm, we went into the garden, and drank tea under the shade of some apple trees, only he and myself. Amidst other discourse, he told me, he was just in the same situation as, when formerly, the notion of gravitation came into his mind. 'Why should that apple always descend perpendicularly to the ground,' thought he to himself, occasioned by the fall of an apple, as he sat in a contemplative mood. 'Why should it not go sideways, or upwards, but constantly to the earth's center? Assuredly, the reason is that the earth draws it. There must be a drawing power in matter'" (spelling and punctuation modernized).

WebExhibits. "Newton and the Color Spectrum," *Color Vision and Art* (webexhibits.org/colorart/bh.html). A fascinating, accessible exploration of Newton's experiments and emerging theories about light and color.

White, Michael, *Isaac Newton: The Last Sorcerer* (New York: Basic Books, 1999).